Fireplaces

Fireplaces

Architecture and Design

Encarna Castillo

HARPER
DESIGN
international

An Imprint of HarperCollins*Publishers*

Editor in Chief: **Haike Falkenberg**

Editor: **Encarna Castillo**

Text: **Sarah Martin Pearson**

Art Director: **Mireia Casanovas Soley**

Graphic Design and Layout: **Ignasi Gracia Blanco**

Research: **Marta Casado**

Corrections: **Susana González**

First published in 2004 by:
Harper Design International,
An imprint of HarperCollins Publishers
10 East 53rd Street
New York, NY 10022
Tel: (212) 207-7000
Fax: (212) 207-7654
HarperDesign@harpercollins.com
www.harpercollins.com

Distributed throughout the world by:
HarperCollins International
10 East 53rd Street
New York, NY 10022
Fax: (212) 207-7654

HarperCollins books may be purchased for educational, business, or sales promotional use. For information, please write: Special Markets Department, HarperCollins Publishers Inc., 10 East 53rd Street, New York, NY 10022

Library of Congress Cataloging-in-Publication Data

Fireplaces : architecture and design / edited by Encarna Castillo.
    p. cm.
 ISBN 0-06-074793-5 (hardcover)
 1. Fireplaces. I. Castillo, Encarna.
 NA3050.F575 2004
 721'.8--dc22

                            2004002403

Editorial Project:
2003 © LOFT Publications
Via Laietana 32, 4° Of. 92
08003 Barcelona. Spain
Tel.: +34 932 688 088
Fax: +34 932 687 073
loft@loftpublications.com
www.loftpublications.com

Printed by Anman Gràfiques del Vallès, Spain

DL: B-17.897-04
First Printing, 2004

CONTENTS

INTRODUCTION 8

THE HISTORY OF FIREPLACES 12

PRACTICAL INFORMATION 26

What You Should Know 29
Types of Fireplaces 33
General Advice 37

MODELS OF FIREPLACES 40

Finishes 42
- Stone
- Marble
- Wood
- Brick
- Metal
- Parget
- Tiles
Positioning 86
- Freestanding Fireplaces
- Built-in Fireplaces and Fireplaces Against a Wall
- Combination Fireplaces
Style 106
- Rustic
- Classical
- Modern
- Minimalist
- Maximalist
- Beach
- City
- Mountain
Outdoor Fireplaces 156
Bibliography 174

INTRODUCTION

The historical relationship between mankind and fire is rife with profound symbolism. The struggle to gain control of the forces of nature arises from our instinct to survive. It could be said that by controlling fire we conquer the potential fury of its flames, allowing us to enjoy its benefits and to avoid its destructive abilities. Controlling fire permitted us to introduce fire into our everyday lives and make it a part of our home, first as open fires that scared off wild animals, and later as a means for cooking. It also became a source of heat, in the form of a hearth and chimney. However, in our drive toward progress we have made technological innovations that have sidelined the hearth-chimney as a basic necessity and have reduced them to merely a domestic comfort of secondary importance. Nevertheless, the fireplace has not lost its symbolic role, and nowadays it is shrouded in romanticism.

In the last few years fireplaces have seen unprecedented developments, both aesthetically and functionally, and they now come in models suited to all types of settings and styles. They help create charming, imaginary microcosms that conjure up coziness and relaxation, to be enjoyed alone or with our loved ones. They evoke profound feelings of home and are imbued with sweet nostalgia.

This book aims to provide an introduction to the world of fireplaces from the viewpoint of contemporary architecture and interior design, as well as explore various themes from a practical and aesthetic angle. This volume is illustrated with captivating photographs that convey the diversity of approaches to fireplace design, in line with current trends. Hopefully this work will serve as both a visual and conceptual reference book for the design of fireplaces, now and in the future.

©Pere Peris

The History of Fireplaces

The History of Fireplaces

It is difficult to pinpoint exactly when the fireplace emerged as an integral part of the home. However, it goes without saying that the cultural development of mankind is closely linked to the use of fire, which played a key role in the history of progress.

The first known evidence of fireplaces—at least in the form recognized today—dates back to the twelfth century. As far as we know, they did not exist in ancient times. The Romans, however, did use an underground heating system based on pipes containing water, which was heated by means of enclosed, coal-burning braziers. It is known that both Greek and Roman houses had an open hole in the ceiling that allowed smoke to escape from hearths and kitchens and could usually be closed with a kind of valve. The Romans used the word *caminus* indiscriminately for both a hearth and a fire for burning wood, as well as for a blacksmith's forge or a furnace for smelting metals. Some of these furnaces and hearths must have had a tube-like shaft for the extraction of smoke, as archeological remains of these constructions have been found. Similarly, Greek vases and Egyptian paintings depict ovens with chimneys, but these mainly served for cooking. Chimneys are not known to have been used in connection with heating until the beginning of the Christian era.

At the start of the Middle Ages the first fireplaces were circular and had a semi-conical extractor hood with a tube leading from the hearth into the wall. From the twelfth century onward, rectangular fireplaces with pyramidal hoods were built and, if the walls were not too thick, the smoke was ventilated through to the exterior.

The story of the Anglo-Saxon fireplace model boasts some of the most extensive documentation in this field. We have therefore taken English fireplaces as a descriptive example, as they probably exerted a considerable influence on the rest of the Western world and they provide numerous clues to the development of this domestic component. However, even in England, and until well into medieval times, we can only find mention of open fires on the ground in the middle of a dwelling. In both circular huts and rustic medieval houses, the fumes were vented by way of a simple opening in the ceiling.

The proliferation of stone fortresses with wooden floorboards in twelfth-century England made it necessary to move the hearth from the middle of the floor and place it against a wall, where it became incorporated into the structure of the load-bearing walls. For the first time, fire hoods began to be placed over the hearth. These were made of stone and were free of any type of ornamentation, as they were purely functional. The only decoration at this time was reserved for the cylindrical shafts that came out of the roof, which were crowned with stylish hoods (similar to the caps used nowadays). These not only afforded protection from rain but they were also fitted with holes that provided shelter from the wind and avoided problems with cross currents. This is the true origin of the chimney as we know it today, although its design and form would continue to evolve as new solutions were found for the problem of extracting smoke. The Normans, however, decided to remove the kitchen from the rest of the dwelling, because of the excessive heat and smoke inside their houses, and place it in a separate building, with its own cooking fires.

At this point we begin to see two parallel developments. The wealthy classes in Britain, influenced by their relationship with France, adopted the Norman model, which was built into the wall and required specialized labor, making it more costly. Furthermore, its location in the exterior wall of a building increased fuel consumption. Aristocrats gradually started to place the smoke chambers on the inside of the wall, and they went on to use stone rather than brick for their construction. It was not until the fourteenth century that fireplaces began to be decorated, originally with shields and bas-reliefs on the jambs, panels, and trimmings. Later, the Gothic splendor of the early fifteenth century ushered in exquisite craftsmanship and an unprecedented decoration of the mouth of the fireplace.

At the other extreme, the lower classes opted for a return to the traditional medieval hearth of Saxon origin. It was cheaper to build, used less fuel and, although it had the drawback of less efficient smoke elimination, it was safer in rural English houses with wooden rafters. Over time, the main change in these fireplaces would be the introduction of brickwork and the fitting of a fire hood, and as a result they had to be built into a wall that was specially constructed to accommodate them. This development marked the appearance of the chimney corner, the so-called inglenook. The nook resulting from the addition of this wall created the effect of extending the mouth of the fireplace, which allowed people to "get inside it." The inglenook was a symbol of medieval times and later would become a source of inspiration for the Arts and Crafts movement.

Around the sixteenth century, English houses started to incorporate a second floor. Fireplaces were installed on this floor as well, and shared a common chimney structure, both vertically and horizontally, marking the beginning of the combination fireplace. Brick became the favored construction material and replaced the hitherto traditional stone and wood. Coal was introduced for burning; it was a much more efficient source of energy but it worsened the smoke problem. Consequently, a great effort was made to improve the extraction of fumes. Once this was perfected, and combustion efficiency was improved, the conditions became ripe for the return of the kitchen to the interior of the home. In this period the built-in fireplace gained such prestige and importance

©Montse Garriga

©Montse Garriga

that it became an entity in its own right, giving rise to an influx of experienced craftsmen from Flanders, Italy, and Germany, who developed the decorative work on the mouth of fireplaces. They recreated the most diverse architectural styles, which would only rarely coincide with the design of the houses in which they were set. For the first time, the fireplace was seen as a feature to be displayed rather than a mere structural element.

The seventeenth century witnessed great changes in the interior layout of houses, and the architect became increasingly important. The differences between the medieval fireplace, attached to a wall, and the typically aristocratic built-in fireplace, began to be blurred and took on merely aesthetic rather than social connotations. The Renaissance and the return to classical architectural canons created a dilemma with respect to the external appearance of a fireplace. For the first time, architects seriously thought about the problems of fireplace design and came to consider fireplaces as elements with their own identity. In this period they laid the groundwork for the concepts that are still in vogue in present-day fireplace design. Two major figures stand out in this process.

Inigo Jones (1573-1652) made the fireplace the focal point of the room. He contributed a succession of superimposed frames on the mouth of the fireplace, which was crowned with a panel of stone or cut marble and a mantelpiece made from a less costly material.

Sir Christopher Wren (1632-1723) integrated the fireplace into the overall look of the room so that it no longer stood out as the focus of attention. He unified the upper pediment and the side walls by means of wood paneling, while framing the mouth with simple molding. Other common distinguishing features in his designs were the placement of a mirror on the upper panel and a series of tiered mantelpieces on which pottery could be displayed. He borrowed the French corner fireplace model, even though its practicality falls far short of its visual appeal.

In the seventeenth century, especially in the homes of the well-to-do, it became common to design bedrooms with a fireplace. Around this time the fireplace started to be considered a symbol of comfort rather than a basic necessity.

The eighteenth century saw the coming of the Industrial Revolution, accompanied by the rise of the middle class and the development of the construction industry. The first mass-produced houses were built, along with their corresponding standardized fireplaces. Aristocratic circles began to disseminate style manuals intended to educate the general public about aesthetics. The fireplace built into the wall became the norm, and hearths in the middle of a room were seen as relics of the past and vestiges of poverty. The appearance of fireplaces continued to be of concern to architects and designers until the arrival of the Adams brothers. They formulated new concepts, including a symmetrical opening that was elaborately decorated with a marble or stone bas-relief frame, an upper mantelpiece for decorative articles, and a panel integrated into the wall, on which a painting could be hung. From then on, the development of the fireplace would go hand in hand with technological advances; as far as the design was concerned, this was dominated by successive revivals of past styles, which were often mixed indiscriminately. As a result, craftsmen were frequently forced to produce endless series of replicas, which choked their creative impulses.

Throughout the nineteenth century there was an insatiable series of revivals, before the neo-romantic movement began to search for a fireplace with a distinct identity and came up with a model made of cast iron and adorned with ceramic tiles. The emergence of gas and electricity at the end of the century marked the end of the fireplace as a means of heating. Even so, a fireplace was still being placed in every room of a house at the start of the twentieth century, and the new artistic movements continued to embellish this feature with innovative decoration.

Art Nouveau focused its attention on the cast-iron fireplace adorned with tiles, while the Arts and Crafts movement, led by William Morris, reinterpreted the medieval fireplace. Later on, the designs of Charles Rennie Mackintosh, the visionary architect from the

©Montse Garriga

©Montse Garriga

Glasgow school, would try to reconcile the past with the new century. In his aim to grant equal importance to form and function, he incorporated niches and recesses into the geometric lines of his designs, making him a precursor to the minimalism in interior design that would appear 25 years later.

Art Deco emerged after the First World War. It was characterized by an emphasis on function and a subordination of form, a rejection of revivalism in favor of modern aesthetic values and a synthesis of industrialization and design. Experimentation with traditional materials brought new interpretations of the fireplace that reduced the ornamentation but were more innovative and more in tune with the times. Nevertheless, a wide range of revivalist designs continued to be prevalent among the lower and middle classes.

The devastating effects of the Second World War demanded the reconstruction of bombed-out homes. The urgent housing needs of entire families encouraged the spread of prefabricated electric fireplaces, which were quicker and simpler to install. The prosperity of the 1950s resulted in a demand for a variety of housing styles once again, and this progressively increased the demand for fireplaces. In the 1970s this demand peaked, giving rise to a proliferation of the gas fireplaces that had recently come on the market.

In the last thirty years, aesthetic tendencies have developed along similar lines. Fireplaces continue to be adapted to a vast range of styles and are being produced in all kinds of materials, but with more sophisticated construction techniques. Designers have total freedom of creative expression, while manufacturers are continually perfecting the technical aspects of wood-burning, gas, and electric fireplaces. In any case, the fireplace is now more than ever a symbolic element that evokes sensations of comfort and coziness in a home, as its heating efficiency is often questionable. It has thus become a feature that gives us the thrill of lighting a fire in our homes, thereby invoking tradition and the most primitive of human instincts.

Practical Information

Practical Information

What You Should Know

Some important construction requirements:

Bear in mind that both the fireplace and the immediate surrounding area have to be made of fireproof or fire-resistant materials. Concrete, standard or vitrified brick, natural stone, various types of coatings and stuccoes, ceramic slabs, and sheets of copper and iron are the most common. In order to satisfy fire-safety requirements and other construction criteria, it is advisable to refer to the regulations in force in your area with respect to fireplace construction or consult a specialist or professional.

It is important that a fireplace can be maintained easily and thoroughly. Similarly, when a fireplace is not in use, it should be easy to close off, with either a dome damper or a cover on the mouth of the fireplace. Some contemporary designs enable a fireplace to be closed off by means of a glass shield. These and other technical advances also prevent smoke from entering the room, avoiding a considerable health hazard.

The components of the internal structure of a built-in fireplace:

The mouth, or opening, of the fireplace | This is the true fireplace, where the combustion takes place. The size and placement will determine the amount of heat radiation in the room, and also the extent to which the flames can be viewed. It is advisable to search for the ideal configuration for both of these parameters, although the size of the room is the determining factor. A rectangle lying on its side is the ideal shape for the opening. The volume of the room and the size of the chimney shaft will determine the height and width of the opening.

The grate | This is usually made of wrought iron, and the logs to be burned are placed on it. The spacing of the bars should allow only the ashes, not the firewood, to fall through. Furthermore, it must be designed to allow ventilating air to enter—if not, the fire will go out. In old rural hearths the grate was often built into the structure of the fireplace's side walls, but nowadays it is usually a separate, unattached accessory. It is often complemented by andirons, metal braces like little sawhorses, on which the logs are placed.

The ash dump | This is situated under the grate and serves to collect the ashes that result from the combustion. It is usually hidden below the level of the mouth of the fireplace, preferably with a removable drawer, which makes it easier to remove the ashes efficiently.

The entrance of air | This is indispensable for all open fireplaces as it guarantees the optimum combustion. There are different ways of achieving this. One possibility is simply to take advantage of the sealing off of a home's doors and windows from the exterior. Another option is to have gaps that open onto the lower part of the ash dump, but it is best to have shafts going under the floor or through the wall and out to the exterior, which allows air to come in directly.

The fire hood | This extends from the upper edge of the mouth of the fireplace to the smoke chamber. Its purpose is to extract the fumes and prevent them from coming out through the mouth. In built-in fireplaces it is usually set in the wall, whereas in other models, such as wrought-iron fireplaces, it is normally designed to be shown off as an external element. The ideal materials for fire hoods are wrought iron, iron sheets, or firebricks. The shape and placement depend on the position of the smoke pipe, as well as the exterior wall, but the structure is almost always pyramidal in protruding fireplaces and rectangular in built-in ones.

The throat | This runs from the lintel over the mouth of the fireplace and narrows to the dome damper, where it connects with the smoke chamber. The dome damper is normally made of iron; it regulates the passage of smoke and fumes and enlarges or reduces the opening of the throat, blocking the entrance of cold air, which would speed up the combustion and cause heat to be lost into the atmosphere. It is practically indispensable, as it allows the fireplace to be totally closed off when it is not in use. It therefore serves to keep out dust and insects in the summer, and avoid heat loss in the winter. Dome dampers are available in collapsible, revolving, and sliding models.

The smoke chamber | This is a slanted, bag-shaped space following immediately on from the throat of the fireplace, formed from the widening and backward tilt at the end of the smoke pipe. It pools the cold air that enters from above and prevents sudden draughts of cold air from pushing smoke into the room.

The smoke pipe | This is tube-shaped and is the final stage in the smoke extraction system. It narrows up from the smoke chamber and leads to the roof before opening onto the exterior. It is normally crowned with a hood or cap, which sticks out from the roof and provides protection from the rain and inclement weather. The sum of all the parts of the smoke pipe constitutes what is commonly known as the chimney.

Types of Fireplaces

The industrial development of fireplaces has provided various technical advances, especially in regard to different types of combustion and the production of heat, as well as in construction methods. Nowadays, the market offers classic wood-burning fireplaces, which occupy most of the pages in this book, and those that use gas or electricity, and are therefore easier to operate and maintain.

Gas fires tend to favor more sober designs, which makes them ideal for a minimalist design, whereas electric fires are usually limited to recreating the appearance of flames, in a totally harmless but artificial manner, which creates a somewhat sterile effect. Gas fires have advantages—as they use real flames, they provide the feeling of well-being normally associated with fireplaces.

One of the main features of a gas-burning hearth using natural gas, butane, or propane is that it is very economical. The need to supply and store firewood is eliminated in favor of an automated supply of fuel, which does not produce any fumes, smells, or residues, making it more hygienic. As there is no firewood, there is therefore no need for constant supervision—only turn on the gas and leave it burning. Another plus is the formal freedom open to designers, which allows them to depart from conventional models. It is still possible to imitate a traditional open fireplace while avoiding nuisances typically associated with them, but it is also possible to radically transform the concept of a fireplace and choose a more avant-garde approach.

One of the characteristics of this type of hearth is that devices can be inserted in the opening to recreate the appearance of a traditional fireplace. These include wrought-iron grates that conceal the gas pipes and pottery logs that look incredibly real. There are two types of gas hearths—open and closed ones. The latter imitate old-fashioned cast-iron stoves; they comprise a closed iron box, which can only be opened at the front, and a metal shell that takes maximum advantage of the heat radiation.

Let us return to traditional **wood-burning fireplaces**. It is important to be aware of the different types of wood that can be burned, as their qualities vary in accordance with their origin. The choice of a particular type of wood can control factors such as the amount of heat and the intensity generated, and the noise and the smell when it burns. Two types of wood are usually distinguished: hard and soft. Hard wood has a gentle flame and produces little ash. Trees that provide good hard wood are maple, acacia, beech, holm oak, oak, and fruit trees; soft woods include chestnut, birch, pine, poplar, fir, and elm. These are characterized by a lively flame and an abundance of ash. Furthermore, they have the disadvantage of burning more quickly and shooting off sparks when they are resinous.

Firewood should be stored in an environment that matches its own level of humidity, since it will burn too fast if it dries out. Finally, it is advisable to use long logs and place them in the fire correctly, in flat layers or at angles, and preferably on top of andirons, which guarantee the oxygenation of the flames.

An open fireplace requires constant supervision—not only for safety reasons, but also to ensure optimum combustion and to regulate the flames. Various auxiliary utensils are available for this task. Some of the most common instruments are tongs for handling the logs, a broom, a dustpan for removing coal and ashes, and bellows for blowing in air to get a fire going again. Furthermore, it is advisable to make use of a screen to prevent accidents from flying sparks. In order to store the firewood in a suitable place, it is useful to use boxes or baskets, or even to incorporate a firewood storage space into the design of the fireplace, such as a hollow space in the wall, or a shelf, or something similar. Other useful complements include utensils for cooking over a fire, such as grates, rotisseries, supports for pans and skillets, and chains for hanging pots and kettles.

General Advice

Before designing a fireplace, the decor of the room where it is to be placed should be considered, since the style must fit in harmoniously with the overall look. All colors, materials and shapes must be totally integrated into the whole. It is advisable to ensure good visibility for the flames, in order to fully enjoy the light and heat of the fire. Lastly, the placement of the fireplace with respect to the surrounding elements and the distribution of the furniture around it must also be taken into account. The chapter on fireplace models presents various ways to site a fireplace in a room, but first we shall focus on the distribution of the furniture, particularly the seating.

If the room is designed solely for the use of the fireplace, the placement of the furniture is simple, as the fireplace takes center stage. A single functional area arranged around the fireplace is the key to this type of distribution. On the other hand, if the fireplace is part of a room that's divided into several areas, a balance needs to be struck so that the fireplace is the focal point when the fire is lit but merges into the setting when not in use. In this case, the placement of the furniture is multidirectional, even though this may cause interference between the different functional areas. The aim here is that the field of vision from the seating is diversified when the fire is not lit and goes beyond the simple dark hollow of the hearth. So, the seating serves primarily as functional living-room furniture, and only secondarily as vantage points for contemplating the fireplace. In both cases, however, it is advisable to make the visibility of the flames and the warmth as similar as possible for all the seating. The furnishing around a fireplace can be characterized by a radial, transversal, or frontal distribution.

Radial | If the fireplace is placed in the center, or is isolated and set off to the side, the most common way to distribute the seating is in a circle or polygon, either by way of benches or individual seats. If the fireplace is sunk into the floor, cushions placed around it will serve as informal seating. This would be a typical example of unidirectional distribution that places full emphasis on the fireplace.

Transversal | A transversal distribution in respect to the mouth of the fireplace favors visual communication with the other functional elements of the room. This layout allows the flames to be contemplated while at the same time keeping other horizontal visual viewpoints open for enjoyment. The major drawback is that the most distant seats receive significantly less warmth.

Frontal | By placing the seating in front of the fireplace we can ensure that its warmth reaches all the seats, with the best possible view of the flames. This is a good solution for fireplaces with several sides, or those placed in a corner. In the latter case, it is advisable to enrich the field of vision, which has been reduced by the corner placement. This can be done with elements like shelves, which complement the panel above the mantelpiece.

Bear in mind that when the fireplace is not in use for extended periods of time, such as in the summer, it can become a sterile void or a nuisance, but it can be transformed by adding decorative elements according to taste. A few suggestions are plants, candles, stones, or unusually shaped logs. All of these can be good substitutes for the focus of attention provided by a blazing fire.

Models of Fireplaces

©Montse Garriga

Finishes

A wide variety of materials can be used for building a fireplace. It goes without saying that the majority are fireproof, which is important due to the proximity of the flames. The only exception is wood. Though wood can be made to be fire resistant, it is generally only used for the exterior finish of the fireplace to avoid direct contact with the flames.

In the section that follows, the emphasis is on the exterior finishes. The materials that can serve as an ideal basis for the construction of the fireplace are highlighted. Some of the most commonly used materials follow.

©Matteo Piazza

Stone | Nature has provided us with myriad types of stone, whose physical characteristics vary according to their mineral composition, which in turn determine the external features of color, texture, and hardness. Some types of stone can even vary in appearance in accordance with their geographical origins. A wide variety of natural stones are ideally suited to the exterior of a fireplace, especially limestone, sandstone, granite, slate, and marble, which will be discussed in a separate section. Limestone is rather delicate, due to its great porosity, but it is one of the most elegant stones for cladding, benches, and flooring. Sandstone can be cut into blocks to make rustic fireplaces. Slate adds a rural touch since it is often used to cover the roofs of houses in the mountains, and is often associated with wood-burning hearths. Today, there are various types of artificial stones on the market that are industrially manufactured from mineral conglomerates. Of these, concrete is one of the most important for both building and finishing fireplaces; it is often used to attain a purely functional fireplace with a robust, industrial look.

©Montse Garriga

©Montse Garriga

©Montse Garriga

Marble | This material deserves is own section, due to the incredible variety of marbles available, as well as the long tradition of use in the mouth of fireplaces. A synonym for luxury and sophistication, marble is normally used for classical fireplaces and is often carved with bas-reliefs or decorative motifs reminiscent of ancient architectural styles. However, the aesthetic qualities of marble are also inspiring more contemporary interpretations of the fireplace, with Travertine being one of the most popular types used. For the classical versions, red, brown, emerald-green, black, and white marbles with minimal grain are particularly prized, although modern interior design is gradually adopting these and many other types of marble to formulate new interpretations of the fireplace and forge a new aesthetic idiom.

© Duccio Malagamba

© Tuca Reinés

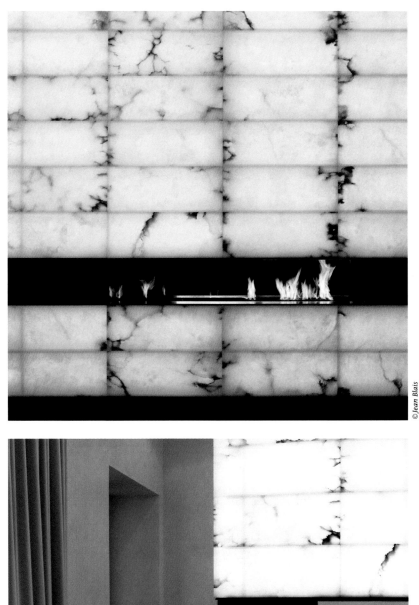

©Jean Blais

©Jean Blais

Wood | As mentioned earlier, wood is flammable and so requires special treatment. Its use is restricted to cladding, often in the form of panels on the front of the fireplace. It is also often used to make ledges or custom-made shelves and closets on the front and sides. In one of its most traditional applications, it is used for molding to frame the mouth of the fireplace or, in a more rustic vein, a beam can be incorporated for use as a mantelpiece. Wood can even be used for making side jambs.

©Montse Garriga

©Tatiana Brockmann

©Ricardo Labougle

©Montse Garriga

©Hergóm

©Hergóm

Brick | Firebricks are ideal for building fireplaces due to their exceptional fireproofing characteristics. However, standard brick can also be used for the exterior cladding to create a "half-finished" look, and to give the impression that a fireplace is made entirely of brick. Fireplaces finished in this way can have either an urban or a rustic appearance, depending on the type of brick and the formal composition of the ensemble. Bricks can be made by hand or manufactured industrially; handmade bricks convey an appealing rural feel, as they are considered to be more authentic and are rougher and often irregular, whereas industrial bricks, with their more urban look and uniform coloring, are rectilinear and smooth. Even though classic red bricks are the most familiar, bricks also come in other colors, such as yellow, white, and brown. White brick, for example, lends a Mediterranean touch, making it the ideal material for a fireplace in a beach house.

©Montse Garriga

©Montse Garriga

©Ricardo Labougle

©Montse Garriga

Metal | Metal can be extremely striking in a fireplace. The most common types are cast iron, stainless steel, and copper. Cast iron is the most suitable for monolithic fireplaces, cast in a single piece. These can be placed next to a wall, or they can be freestanding. This material can be left bare—although it is often painted a dark color—to emphasize its stark physical presence and allow the essential elements of the fireplace to stand out. Its character, totally free of any ornamentation, makes this kind of fireplace highly adaptable to all styles and settings. Stainless steel is also used for monolithic fireplaces, although it can merely be used, like copper, for cladding the exterior or for a fire hood.

©John Linkins / Brit Andersen

©Eugeni Pons

©Ricardo Labougle

Parget | The exterior of fireplaces made from cement conglomerates or bricks can be coated with plaster, which softens the contours and unifies the ensemble by endowing it with an impeccable white finish. There are pure "Ibiza"-style versions of this type of fireplace, characterized by the formal sinuosity of their contours and whimsical lines. There are also more sophisticated models with bare surfaces and geometric forms, free of all ornamentation, in the purest of minimalist styles. A similar option is a stucco finish, which is very common in built-in fireplaces. Although white is by far the most popular color, both plaster and stucco can be tinted with paints and pigments to attain other colors.

©Ricardo Labougle

©Philippe Saharoff

©Montse Garriga

Tiles | Tiles are very durable and have excellent fireproofing qualities. The Art Nouveau movement first used tile to cover fireplaces in combination with wrought iron, creating beautiful tiled mosaics that were finely decorated and painted by hand. Catalan Modernism, inspired by the Middle Eastern designs, also made use of tiles, for both chimneys and fireplaces, which were often entirely covered with small tiles in a style known as *trencadís*. Some of the most famous examples are the chimneys designed by Antonio Gaudí for the top of the Casa Milà in Barcelona. Tiles are also commonly used in closed wood-burning stoves, as they retain heat very efficiently. These days, tiled craftwork with hand-painted designs has found another outlet, on the upper panel above the mantelpiece.

©Gordon H. Schenk

©Gordon H. Schenk

©Pere Planells

©Pere Planells

Positioning

The placement of the fireplace is a determining factor in the spatial organization of a room, whether a living room, a kitchen, a bedroom, a library, or even a garden (in the case of a barbecue pit). As the hub of the room, the position of a fireplace will have a decisive influence on the layout of the furniture and the other functional areas. There are various layout plans to choose from, depending on the type of fireplace.

©Hélène Binet

Freestanding Fireplaces | A freestanding fireplace is set up on its own, in a more or less central position. It can be located in the center of the room, in a corner, or in front of a wall. If it is in the garden, it should be next to the house or in a spot that provides protection from the wind. It contains a single fire but may have one, two, three, or four sides with an opening. The smoke outlet can be behind, on top of, or on the side of the fireplace.

©Montse Garriga

©Ricardo Labougle

©José Manuel Bielsa

©Montse Garriga

©Montse Garriga

Built-in Fireplaces and Fireplaces Against a Wall | These are attached to

or built into a wall, or suspended in front of a wall; they can also be found in the form of a wall hearth or a block hearth. They normally contain only one fire, but there may be an opening on one, two, or even three sides. As with freestanding fireplaces, the smoke outlet can be behind, on top of, or on the side of the fireplace.

©Montse Garriga

©Michael Weschler

Combination Fireplaces | These take advantage of one common chimney structure but contain two, or sometimes even three, fires. They can form a self-contained block or be attached to or built into the wall. They can have openings on different sides of a same room, or in different adjoining rooms or spaces. Similarly, an interior fireplace may open onto the exterior as a barbecue attached to or built into the wall, or even in some cases through a window. It is common for the fires to be next to or behind each other, although in houses with more than one floor they can even be on top of one another. The mouth of the fireplace can open out on one, two, or three sides. As with the previous two types of fireplaces, the smoke outlet can be behind, on top of, or on the side of the fireplace.

©Eduardo Consuegra

©Eduardo Consuegra

Style

Over the course of time, the appearance of fireplaces has successively absorbed a host of artistic trends and architectural styles especially since the fourteenth century, when interest in decorating fireplace jambs, walls, and trimmings grew. A categorization of styles based on traditional models follows, seeking to throw light on modern trends in interior decoration with regard to fireplaces and in fireplace design in general.

©Adriano Brusaforri

Rustic | As the name indicates, this style of fireplace can be found in a country home or recreated in a different setting. It is characterized by the use of natural materials whose color and texture are unaltered, such as unpolished stone, handmade bricks, or wooden beams. Often this rustic style is accentuated by the use of decorative accessories that aim to bring out its rural character, like pans, handcrafted tiles, and garden produce such as ears of corn, garlic heads, or pumpkins that can be hung on the front panel. This style is frequently found in vacation homes, although it is not uncommon in primary residences in urban areas.

©Montse Garriga

©Pere Planells

Classical | This term usually refers to fireplaces with a traditional design that recreates decorative motifs drawn from ancient Greek or Roman architectural styles, though with a degree of artistic license. The decoration is usually focused on the frame surrounding the mouth of the fireplace, where polished stone, normally marble or granite, is the most common material. The fireplace is usually partially built into a wall, and the mouth is usually flush with the wall, or only slightly protruding. In the most modern versions of this style the ornamentation is kept to a minimum. Recent variations have introduced a frame around the mouth made of plaster or sculpted wood, which is then painted, often with bright colors, to create a highly modern effect that can be very striking in eclectic interiors.

©Montse Garriga

©Montse Garriga

©Jordi Miralles

©Carlos Dominguez

©Montse Garriga

©Farshid Assassi

©Hergóm

©Andreas J. Focke

©Virginia del Guidice

©Undine Pröhl

©Undine Pröhl

©Stefan Müller

Minimalist | Minimalism in present-day architecture and interior design is an aesthetic approach that seeks order, equilibrium, and the essence of form, which is here interlinked with function. It eliminates as much ornamentation as possible, and is characterized by an almost total absence of color and the use of fine materials applied with the utmost sobriety. It is based on ancient Asian philosophies that focus on tranquility, equilibrium, and inner peace. A minimalist space can convey a deep sense of peace since it seems that absolutely nothing occurs in its bare interior. However, contrary to appearances, the minimalist style demands a lot of work from a functional point of view, as it requires a search for the utilitarian and formal essence of objects. Thus, the epitome of a minimalist fireplace could be one that has, as its only visible element, a fire in its mouth, complemented by a clean interplay of pure forms, with all the entire inner mechanisms of the fireplace hidden from view. The composition and the intersection of planes would be freely fashioned by the designer to achieve the desired formal effects.

©Montse Garriga

©Eduardo Consuegra

©Andrew Bordwin Studio

Maximalist | The maximalist style, the opposite of minimalism, creates over-elaborate and highly adorned settings with objects of diverse origins. This style is based on cultural, formal, and material eclecticism. Its expressiveness is boundless, almost theatrical, and it revels in an array of textures, bright colors, fine materials, and a touch of kitsch. When this style is applied to fireplaces, the result is often a revision and reinterpretation of classical styles with abundant doses of creativity.

©Pep Escoda

© Yael Pincus

© Deidi von Schaewen / Omnia

136 **Fireplaces**

©Ricardo Labougle

Beach | Although this is not a style per se, this heading groups together the fireplaces found in houses by the sea. The aim is to avoid clichés and examine how the fireplace is interpreted in this style of decor. Some of the most common examples are included, such as the Ibiza-style fireplace, with an outer coating of undulating plaster, or the Mediterranean-style fireplace, made of white or red brick with touches of rustic wood or a finishing of white stucco.

©Ricardo Labougle

©Melba Levick

©Melba Levick

©Melba Levick

©Montse Garriga

City | The urban setting has become a source of inspiration for fireplace design. A rethinking of the traditional home led to a proliferation of loft-style residences, which had their origin in industrial premises that were converted into domestic habitats. The industrial look of lofts has been a source of inspiration for an urban style of fireplaces. In the most representative models of this style, the most prominent feature is the roughness of bare materials such as brick, concrete, or iron, which are then treated with varying degrees of sophistication. This is not to say that all city fireplaces share these characteristics; just as in many other settings, the varied range of styles of houses in cities and suburbs and the broad range of tastes in their diverse populations give rise to a vast array of interior design styles and, therefore, a wide variety of fireplaces.

©Matteo Piazza

©Wini Sulzbach

©Montse Garriga

©Melba Levick

Mountain | The traditional fireplace in houses in the mountains has much in common with the rustic style. The typical image is that of a huge stone fireplace, perhaps finished with wooden beams. In the mountains, as in the country, a fireplace was traditionally built in the kitchen, which included a dining area, and served as a meeting place for all the family. In this case it was used for cooking, but it was customary to put fireplaces in the other rooms for heating purposes. However, as in the case of beach homes, the aim here is to outline the different types of fireplaces that can be installed in a contemporary mountain residence.

©Nuria Fuentes

©Melba Levick

©Montse Garriga

©Roland Bauer

©Sporthotel Lorünser

©Russel Abraham

©Pere Planells

Outdoor Fireplaces

Exterior fireplaces are commonly referred to as barbecues and are in fact inspired by portable barbecues. They are used almost exclusively for outdoor cooking, especially during the hot months of the year. They evoke a festive or holiday atmosphere and always add charm to a house, as they complement the garden or terrace. Today, barbecues are also available for indoor use.

©Eduardo Consuegra

©Carlos Domínguez

The immensely **popular portable barbecue** generally has a simple design, consisting of a metal box for the fire and a grate for cooking food. It may also include an ash pan, which is sometimes removable. The embers of the fuels used—charcoal or wood—give food a distinctive taste. A portable barbecue normally needs a suitably solid base, in the case of tabletop models, although some have their own legs, or even their own table and legs with rollers.

©Peter Kerze

Outdoor fireplaces or built-in barbecues cannot be moved and come in various models, depending on their size and the materials they're made of. They are normally divided into three groups: simple barbecues (without a hood), standard barbecues, and multifunctional barbecues (of large dimensions). They normally contain the same features as portable barbeques, as well as a smoke hood and a smoke pipe. Whatever model is chosen, it needs to have a solid base made of slabs of stone, cement, artificial stone, or concrete. Furthermore, for safety reasons and to avoid problems with smoke congestion and ventilation, the fireplace should be placed at least twenty feet away from any vertical obstruction (for example, the exterior walls of a house or a tree). When looking for the most suitable barbecue model, bear in mind the use it will be put to, as this will determine the size of the grate and, consequently, the size of the barbecue. Make a realistic calculation of the number of people you will be cooking for and the frequency of use. For example, there are low barbecues that are more economical but are also more inconvenient to use, which would cause problems if used often.

©Chipper Hatter

©Carlos Domínguez

Simple barbecues are usually small and normally have no smoke hood. Prefabricated models are common, usually consisting of a kind of table made of cement conglomerate containing the box for the fire, with the grate on top. They are often enclosed by side panels that provide protection from the wind. The platform-like base can furnish space for storing firewood and perhaps also some cooking utensils. Various models are on the market; most are rectangular, although it is not uncommon to find round barbecues that allow for cooking from different sides.

©Per Bernsten / C. V. Holmebakk

©Pere Planells

Standard barbecues are of medium size and are easily adapted to all sorts of uses. They are all equipped with a fire hood and smoke pipe, and so are not limited to outdoor use but can be installed in any enclosed space. We could say that, of all barbecues, they most closely resemble an indoor fireplace. They can be made of diverse materials, but they are usually made of firebricks and are topped with an iron fire hood, or they are made of one single material, such as cast iron or a fireproof cement conglomerate. One advantage of cement conglomerate is that it can be formed into elaborate shapes. The lower part of the base of these barbecues normally includes several niches and spaces for storing firewood or charcoal, or for holding trays of food during the cooking process.

©Pere Planells

The largest and best-equipped barbecues are **multifunctional** models as, apart from the grate, they also boast a grill and a wood-burning oven. Thus, they are complete barbecue-cookers and are suitable for terraces and gardens, and as well as for interior spaces; they are therefore highly recommended for country homes. Up to three different types of cooking can be undertaken: grilling, roasting in the wood-burning oven, or frying on a stone (which is heated by the grill).

©Hergóm

Various auxiliary elements, complementary tools, and useful devices can be purchased to facilitate cooking and the care and maintenance of a barbecue. These tools are similar to those used for indoor fireplaces. First, it is advisable to have on hand small utensils, such as a tool for handling logs, a dustpan and a broom for cleaning, and a set of multi-use tongs. Second, there are a variety of electric accessories available, which make more cooking techniques possible. Of these, two of the most noteworthy are the electric spit for roasting and the portable grate, both made of stainless steel.

©Pere Planells

©Pere Planells

In the case of barbecues set in a garden or on a terrace, it is advisable to design the decor and choose the furniture with care. The advent of good weather makes it immensely enjoyable to relax in an outdoor dining area equipped with a table and chairs, which can be custom-designed or built-in and made of a combination of brick, stone, concrete or wood, in true country style. Highly attractive, ready-made outdoor furniture is also available. During the day, it is useful to set up a beach umbrella with a solid base to provide shade. To make the most of the night time, it is best to install a lighting system comprising lamps or wall lights. A moonlight dinner eaten around the barbecue on a summer night is even more evocative if it is complemented by the exotic illumination of torcheres stuck in the lawn or in plant pots, topped off with a few candles.

©Pere Planells

©Pere Planells

Book References

Danz, Ernst: *Chimeneas-hogar*. Gustavo Gili. Barcelona, 1964.

De Cusa Ramos, Juan: *Chimeneas*. CEAC. Barcelona, 1983.

De Cusa Ramos, Juan: *Chimeneas, estufas de calor integral y barbacoas*. CEAC. Barcelona, 1997.

McDonald, Roxana: *The Fireplace Book*. The Architectural Press. London, 1984.

VV. AA. *Enciclopedia Universal Ilustrada Europeo-Americana*. Espasa-Calpe, S.A. Madrid, 1989.

Internet References

Big Black Book. The Independent Online Design Source - http://www.BigBlackBook.uk.com

HearthNet - http://www.hearth.com

Marco Fireplace - http://www.marco-fireplace.com

Doors Of London - http://www.doorsoflondon.com

Special thanks to HERGOM, Barcelona, Spain.